THE
EDUCATED OUTLAW

Harvey Lay Murdock

authorHOUSE®

AuthorHouse™
1663 Liberty Drive, Suite 200
Bloomington, IN 47403
www.authorhouse.com
Phone: 1-800-839-8640

First published by AuthorHouse 2/2/2009

ISBN: 978-1-4389-4401-2 (sc)

*Printed in the United States of America
Bloomington, Indiana*

This book is printed on acid-free paper.

DEDICATION

This book is dedicated to the people in my life who helped me

In no particular order, those who are not with us anymore

Larry Reno
Charles Kelly
Josie Bassett
Oran & Vida Curry
Ken & Jean Maughan
Floyd Slater
Charles & Rose Fabrizio
Joseph & Marvel Lay Murdock

There are many many more.
As readers you know who you are

Wild Bunch Country

FOREWORD

What makes a person take on a quest? Sometimes it comes from a monumental event that changes someone's life; sometimes it comes from a passing remark. The latter is the spark that fueled my quest.

At the age of 14 living on a sheep ranch in Hanna Utah, my thoughts were on daily chores and school. In the fall of my fourteenth year I was asked by my father to accompany my uncle to take the lambs to market. My uncle was easily influenced to take more than a few drinks when in town and my father needed me to make sure the sheep were taken care of. I was driving back from town because my uncle was unable to. It was an unpaved, long and bumpy ride. My uncle was in a particularly foul mood on that trip and told me "You'll never amount to a damn thing because your grandfather was an outlaw". I didn't pay a lot of attention to him at first.

I asked my mom what he had meant by that statement. My mother told me that her father, my grandfather, was none other than the outlaw Elzy Lay who rode with the Wild Bunch and was close friends with Butch Cassidy.

A passing remark from a grumpy man has led me on a 65 year quest to find out about my grandfather. I am fortunate enough to have talked personally with people acquainted with my grandfather and other members of the Wild Bunch.

William Ellsworth Lay (Elzy) was born on the 25th of November 1868 in Mount Pleasant, Ohio. He died on the 10th of November 1934 in Glendale, California, just short of his 65th birthday

This is the story of my grandfather Elzy Lay.

How My Journey Began

W hen WOLA (Western Outlaw and Lawmen Association) was established, a special group of people were invited to attend. The gathering was held in the Library at Utah State University in Logan, Utah.

Original core of Wola

Pearl Baker, the noted author of books concerning Robbers Roost, was there. Her family owned the cattle ranch that was known as the Robbers Roost Ranch. Lula Parker Betenson, youngest sister of Butch Cassidy, Marvel Lay Murdock, the daughter of Elzy Lay and Bill Linn, the CEO of the Pinkerton Detective Agency were also present. Bill Linn provided support for the organization both morally and financially. The Pinkerton's were responsible for the name "The Wild Bunch" and from then on the name stuck.

When the movie, Butch Cassidy and The Sundance Kid was released in 1969, it started a whole bunch of interest in the outlaws of the old west after the civil war. The movie was made to entertain and in the opening scene of the movie, there is a disclaimer that appears on the screen "some of this story is true". The part of Butch Cassidy was played by Paul Newman and the part of The Sundance Kid was played by Robert Redford. Butch Cassidy's (Robert Leroy Parker) youngest sister, Lula Parker Betenson and my mother (the daughter of Elzy Lay) Marvel Lay Murdock were both invited to the world premiere of the movie. It was held in the Olympic theatre in Provo, Utah. The premiere may have taken place there because of Redford's association with the town and his Sundance Ski Resort.

I had become acquainted with Mrs. Betenson sometime before, when she was visiting a granddaughter in Salt Lake City, Utah. I was in touch with her and asked if she would go with me to Heber City, Utah and meet my mother. I thought these two ought to become acquainted. I drove Mrs. Betenson to Heber City and enjoyed every minute of the trip. She was in her nineties and just as sharp as a tack. We picked up my mother and I took them to lunch at the Homestead Resort in Midway, Utah. We had a great lunch and a great visit. It was very interesting for me to sit back and listen to these two ladies chat as though they had known each other many years.

At the premier, we sat together and watched the movie. It was full of entertainment! After the movie, Mrs. Betenson and two or three of us were standing around visiting. She asked me, "Why was it called Butch Cassidy & the Sundance Kid? Your grandfather Elzy Lay was by far Butch's best and closest friend." Off the top of my head, I suggested the title Butch Cassidy and the Sundance Kid would probably sell more movie tickets than the title, Butch Cassidy & Elzy Lay. That remark was spontaneous but everyone thought it made sense.

Lula Parker Betenson
at about 80

Marvel Lay Murdock
at 80

When Elzy Lay Left Home

When Lay was a youngster, his closest friend was a kid by the name of Bill McGinnis. His full name was William H. McGinnis. The two were inseparable. They had heard stories about the west, cowboying and glamour as it were. They were very young but decided to leave home because one of them had had a love affair that turned sour.

Bill and Elzy started their journey west into the country around Denver, Colorado. There Bill decided to go back home for one reason or another. His life was rather interesting, because later in life he settled in Colorado and found himself in politics. His ultimate achievement was that he became the elected treasurer of the State of Colorado. His family lived around the community of Wray, Colorado.

The title, 'The Educated Outlaw' is from the book "The Outlaw Trail" by Charles Kelly, wherein he referred to Elzy Lay as the educated outlaw. It is intriguing because Elzy Lay completed school only to the eighth grade. In those days that was a fair accomplishment because our society, our country, our people were more agriculturally oriented. The industrial and business minded attitude came from large cities in the east and later in the west. The economy of the land really was farming, livestock and mining.

Elzy was in the Denver area and for some reason, got into a little tussle with a man who was acting like less than a gentleman with a lady. Lay took it upon himself to straighten the guy out. Consequently, he thought he was going to be arrested and decided to leave the area. He left Denver and went on west to gain employment on the border of Colorado & Utah.

He worked on several ranches and farms putting up hay and doing general farm and ranch work. It was in this area that he met the notorious Matt Warner. Warner had a ranch on Diamond Mountain. Lay worked for him occasionally. He also migrated further west into an area called

Brown's Hole, Brown's Hole is a thirty-seven mile long and narrow stretch of land running along the northwestern corner of Colorado, southwestern Wyoming and the northeastern corner of Utah. It is Brown's Park now but in those days, it was called Brown's Hole, and known for some of its seedy characters.

Brown's Hole got its name from a trapper of the early days. Even before the outlaws and the cattlemen were there, there were trappers. A trapper named Babtista Brown lived there and the area took its name from him.

Lay worked on the Bassett ranch in the Brown's Hole area. It is in that era that Butch Cassidy migrated that way from Telluride, Colorado. Matt Warner and Butch Cassidy had their first episode which was a bank robbery in Telluride. That job was done by Butch, Matt and Matt's shirt tail relative Tom McCarty.

One thing about these small towns along the border of Colorado and Utah would be the considerable mining and farming that took place. Weekends meant one thing, horseracing. There was a great deal of gambling that went along with this. Butch and Matt did their share of gambling on the horses and became pretty good friends. As I said before, Matt had a ranch where Elzy Lay worked for him and came to know Cassidy. Lays' first outlaw episode is as follows.

A merchant from Rock Springs, Wyoming, who was in the clothing business, was forced into bankruptcy. Before the liquidators could take his inventory from him, he actually stole his own property from his store and headed south. Matt and Elzy relieved him of his wares while he was on the run. They had a pretty good time distributing it among the residents of Brown's Hole. There were a few families there around that time. That was the only episode where Matt and Elzy actually worked together on a job to the best of my knowledge.

It was during this time that Lay traveled into Ashley Valley, and once there he went to the Albert Davis home to find work putting up hay. A son of Albert Davis went to work with him and together they worked for various farmers and ranchers in the area. While working together, Lay was invited to the Davis home, where he met Albert's daughter Maude. In every account I have found, they were attracted to each other immediately. Lay was probably in his early twenties at the time. He was a handsome lad and she a striking lass.

About this time in Elzy's life, he became very well acquainted with horses. He didn't break horses, he trained them. As far as I can tell, he trained them in quite a different way than the bronco stompers did. They would beat a horse into submission, breaking it of its bad habits, then teach it habits the owner wanted. Elzy didn't do things

A Young Maude Davis

that way. He did it through training the horse and gaining the trust of the animal. He became very good at this. Later on when he and Butch were together in southern New Mexico, Butch would work for the ranchers as a cowboy and Lay would work training the remuda.

Butch & Elzy

To write a story about Elzy Lay and not feature Butch Cassidy would be very difficult and the reverse is also true. Both were employed by ranchers in and around Brown's Hole. The Green River runs through it and the states of Utah, Colorado, and Wyoming share a common border. This is important because jurisdiction across state lines was always a question. Not many lawmen ventured into the area because of that concern.

My objective is to be as accurate as possible. Butch and Elzy became fast friends; both seemed to have above average intelligence from everything we have been able to put together. They were blamed for many robberies they were not involved in because if the law did not have evidence to the contrary, they would simply accuse the "Wild Bunch". This might be technically correct because the "Wild Bunch" was comprised of many individuals and some of them did pull jobs without Butch and Elzy.

There are two jobs I am sure they were together on, the bank robbery in Montpelier, Idaho on the 13th of August 1896 and the Pleasant Valley Coal Company at Castle Gate, Utah on the 21st of April 1897.

THE MONTPELIER BANK

Butch, Elzy and Bub Meeks went to work for a rancher named Emelle near Cokeville, Wyoming not very far from Montpelier, Idaho. The rancher said these three were the best hands he had ever hired. The ranch was actually managed by the wife while the husband operated his jewelry store in Montpelier.

They would ride into town not only to case the bank but to see where to locate the relay horses for their getaway. Their method was to have horses in good condition and to know how far the horses could run. Because of this practice, the posses never caught up with them. With their relays in place they would be back in Brown's Hole in very short order.

Bub Meeks stayed out on the street while Butch and Elzy were inside the bank relieving the teller by the name of Mr. McIntosh of approximately $7,000.00. The manager of the bank was Mr. Gray. The teller was able to identify Bub Meeks for the authorities but the robbery was successful. The money was to be used to hire an attorney for Matt Warner who had been involved in a claim jumping affair at Dry Fork, north of Vernal, Utah.

Matt was jailed in the Uintah, County Jail and Sheriff Pope, afraid the citizens might take the law into their own hands and lynch Warner, moved him through the Uintah Mountains to the Weber County Jail in Ogden, Utah.

Butch and Elzy hired Attorney Douglas Preston, who later became Attorney General of Wyoming. Butch and Elzy camped outside of Ogden and they were able to deliver a message to Warner that they were ready to attempt to break Warner out. Warner was able to deliver a message to Butch and Elzy that he expected a light sentence and it was not worth the risk. He received a two year sentence and was released from the Utah State

Penitentiary after serving the sentence. He is buried in Price, Utah.

A celebration is held each year in Montpelier to commemorate the robbing of the bank. It is called Butch Cassidy Days. An interesting side note is the Deputy tried to pursue the outlaws on a bicycle, the kind with the very large front wheel and the very small rear wheel. They were not captured.

Meeks was captured due to his involvement in another crime of some kind. He later escaped from jail and in the process, broke his leg. It was later amputated. He was released because the court said "a one legged man was not much of a risk to society. Some of Meek's family is located around Wallsburg, Utah.

Matt Warner

The Bassett Family

In Brown's Hole, one of the most prestigious families were the Bassetts. Sam Bassett went into the area as early as 1851. He was sent to scout the area and settled there. Sam's brother, Herbert and his wife Elizabeth were married in Hot Springs, Arkansas. Herbert was a veteran of the civil war in the Union Army. Elizabeth was from a fine family in Virginia. Herbert's health failed and they came west so he could find an area where he could breathe. He had a severe case of asthma.

On the way west they stopped in Rock Springs, Wyoming and then moved on to Evanston, Wyoming where Herbert worked for about a year.

His brother Sam was in Brown's Hole, they communicated as often as they could. Sam talked Herbert and Elizabeth into moving there.

Herbert and Elizabeth had two children, Eb and Josie prior to living in Brown's Hole. After arriving, Anne Bassett was born and was the first white child born there. Anne was later known as Queen Anne .

Both Elizabeth and Herb were very strong in their educational backgrounds. Herb had taught school and he saw to it that the children got an education in a very wild area.

Anne was sent to a finishing school in the east when she became a young lady and Josie was sent to school at St. Mary's of the Wasatch in Salt Lake City. While Anne was at her eastern school, she was in an equestrian class where the ladies who rode horses would do so side saddle. To straddle a horse cowboy style for a lady in those days was unheard of. There was an incident where her instructor was called into the office for a moment and while he was gone, Anne, who was raised riding like a cowboy, got on her horse cowboy style gave a war whoop and entertained the other girls. When the instructor returned and witnessed the folly, he saw to it that Anne was sent home for that breach of etiquette.

When I met Josie, she was in her eighties. Her command of the English language, sense of humor and memory were all amazing. She grew up in Brown's Hole and left there as an adult to homestead in a little place called Cub Creek, north of Jensen, Utah. She lived there for over fifty years and lived the kind of life she wanted. Her reputation was not good. Divorces in those days were not as common as they are now. Josie had five husbands and for various reasons, each ended in separation due to divorce or death.

In the late 1950's and early 60's, I was living in Salt Lake City, Utah with my family. I was in the investment business for most of my life and had a great clientele in Vernal, Utah. I knew about Josie Bassett Morris for some time. One evening, I was sitting in a tavern on the east end of Vernal. The bartender was moon lighting. His real job was as a park ranger for Dinosaur National Monument. He and I were visiting and Josie's name came up. He drew a map on a bar napkin for me that showed how to get to her place. One of the things I am thankful for is I did not procrastinate trying to find her.

Josie's son Crawford McKnight was working in a service station in Jensen. I stopped to meet him and told him who I was and became casually acquainted with him. From there I went across the Green River Bridge going east from Jensen and immediately turned north onto a road that was little more than a cow trail. There were car tracks so I figured I was on the right path according to the map drawn for me.

The road was not well marked. I came to a barbed wire fence with a barbed wire gate. The sagebrush was ten to twelve feet tall which is an indication of really good soil. I was pretty well convinced that I was lost when I got out of the car to look at what was a pasture beyond the fence. There was a three foot blow snake under the fence. That changed my mind about going that direction. As I was backing to turn around to head back to town, I noticed car tracks on the corner. I followed them and turned into the yard of Josie Bassett Morris.

There she was, standing barely five feet tall wearing a slouched brown hat and a pair of bib over-alls that were too big for her. I really didn't know what type of

The Bassett cabin in Brown's Hole

woman I was going to meet. I heard that she had run off one of her husband's with a 30-30 rifle. I didn't know if I might get the same treatment! I stopped, opened the car door and got out. "You must be Josie Bassett Morris" is the way my part of the conversation started. "I am and may I ask your name?" I said "my name is Harv Murdock". She asked "are you of the Murdock's that are sheep people from around Heber City?" "I certainly am but I think you know my mother's side of the family better than you would the Murdock's." I then asked "Did you ever know a man known as Elzy Lay?" She looked at me for 10 to 15 seconds although it seemed longer, I could only guess what might be going through her mind. "Yes, you must be Marvel's boy." "Yes", I answered.

Josie Bassett in front of her cabin in 1963. she was 89

She asked me to come into her home and speak with her. She then proceeded to say "I would like you to know that Elzy Lay was the finest gentleman I ever had the pleasure of knowing". This began a friendship I have treasured since that day.

As I said before, she was so articulate in her speech, and her command of the English language coupled with a keen sense of humor made our conversations rich and fulfilling. Her father made certain that she and her sister Anne received a sound education.

Their Mother, Elizabeth, took charge of the ranch and its business. She fought with the big cattle ranchers until the time of her passing, much too early, I might add. Survival in the business was tough because the big outfits felt the open range belonged to them. Because of that the small ranchers ran into any number of challenges including their stock being run off from water and grazing, the ever present rustling problem and all around bullying.

Anne married Hy Bernard, the manager of one of the bigger ranches which may have been quite interesting in its own right. Charles Kelly, the author of the first book about the "Wild Bunch and Brown's Hole", wrote in the book some not so complimentary things about the Bassett sisters. Anne, who was living in Leeds, Utah with her second husband Frank Willis at the time, drove to Salt Lake City to straighten Mr. Kelly out. As it happened, the peace pipe was smoked and Kelly revised his writing to a more accurate and even complimentary account of the Bassett sisters.

Charles Kelly and I became friends; we spoke often and on one occasion I took my mother to visit. I asked on one of my visits if he had ever met Josie and he replied "No by God, I was afraid she might shoot me". When Charley was gathering information for his book there were no computers or television and radio and telephone service was not always reliable. It was all leg work, and a lot of people would not speak with him because many friends or relatives were still very much alive and accurate information was difficult to come by. He is still regarded as the cornerstone of Western Outlaw History. To leave the story of Josie Bassett without mentioning these incidents would be remiss.

There is a school of thought that Butch Cassidy and the Sundance Kid died around 1909 and are buried in South America. The Pinkerton Detective Agency of that day would have been glad if Butch Cassidy had met his demise in South America because they tried and failed to apprehend him all over the west and South America. I do not subscribe to this theory.

Josie saw Elzy and Butch in 1929 in Rock Springs, Wyoming at the boarding house she managed for Tom Vernon, the owner. Vernon visited Elzy and Butch there and they had drinks together. Mr. Vernon said "if Butch had been killed in South America, the ghost he had a drink with was very active". Josie saw them again in 1932 at the hotel in Baggs, Wyoming. She also managed that business for Tom Vernon. Clint Vernon of that family would later become Attorney General of Utah during the

Anne Bassett Willis 1943

Josie and Anne Bassett over the years

administration of Governor J. Bracken Lee (1949-1957). Mr. Vernon was instrumental in the early

22

days of the National Outlaw and Lawmen Association (NOLA).

Josie and I visited when I could get to see her and we would talk of the Wild Bunch days. She told me she and her sister had dated Butch and Elzy in the early years and the arguments she had with Anne maybe had to do with those relationships.

One year at Christmas, Crawford McNight, Josie's son, traveled to Cub Creek to pick up his mother for the holiday. Josie had a playful colt that knocked her down and the fall broke Josie's hip, she was able to pull herself into the cabin and survived the night. Crawford found her and was able to get her to the hospital in Salt Lake City. She returned from the hospital and was living with Crawford in Jensen, Utah. She was able to get around with an aluminum walker. I visited her that in April of that year.

Many times I told my mother about Josie and suggested they should meet. In May of that year, I took my mother to Vernal, Utah to visit Josie only to find out she had gone to Salt Lake City for a checkup. I sent mom back to Heber City while I stayed in Vernal to work. When I arrived home,

I checked the mail and the newspaper and saw Josie's obituary.

She was one of the most interesting people I have ever met.

THE CASTLE GATE PAYROLL ROBBERY,
THE PLEASANT VALLEY COAL COMPANY
APRIL 21, 1897

This episode was arguably the most carefully planned and near perfectly executed in the history of western outlaws. Butch and Elzy agreed that one of the key elements of any heist was the escape plan.

They knew that solid, well trained horses were essential. They knew how far a horse could run at a fast pace, over hard terrain. At those points, the relays of top horses were placed. By the time a posse was formed to pursue, the outlaws were already on fresh horses and the posse was on spent animals. The chase was over at this point until the posse could obtain fresh animals, and then it would be tracking the bandits, instead of chasing them. They used the same strategy in Montpelier, Idaho and it worked well.

For the Castle Gate job, a large gray horse was obtained from Joe Meeks who had a ranch near Huntington, Utah. Joe was a brother of "Bub" Meeks who was with Butch and Elzy in the Montpelier, Idaho bank robbery. This horse was taken to Mr. Neibauer's ranch. Neibauer, an Austrian and an outstanding horseman, some twenty years earlier, was a messmate of the Arch Duke Rudolph of Austria during his period of compulsory military service. He became the "caretaker" of the Duke's son, the Prince. The Prince became enamored with a woman but something went wrong and in 1889, he committed suicide. To prevent this fact from becoming known, The Prince's messmates were accused of murder and executed with the exception of Neibauer, who escaped one night, taking only what he could carry with him on horseback. It should be noted at this time that among his other activities, Neibauer was a trainer of the famous Lipizzaner Stallions. Neibauer made it to America and then west to Bingham, Utah where he worked in the mines for several years. He contracted rheumatism and was forced to quit. He relocated to a small ranch near Price,

Utah where he became acquainted with Butch and Elzy who called him the "Dutchman". One day Cassidy came to Neibauer's ranch leading a beautiful gray horse. Butch asked him to keep the horse, feed him well and keep him in the corral. In about a week Butch retrieved the animal, and soon after the Castle Gate robbery took place. "Long Brown" was owned by Neibauer and was also acquired by Lay and Cassidy for the Castle Gate job.

Butch was released from the Wyoming State Penitentiary on the 6th of January 1896, where he had served eighteen months of a two year sentence for horse theft. He and Elzy went to work on ranches in the Huntington, Utah area as they had done in Idaho for the Montpelier job. They were planning a big pay day and this was how they staked out the area and became familiar faces.

They considered robbing the fund transfer from Price, Utah to Fort Duchesne to the Ute tribe and other government agencies. This transfer was escorted by a U. S. cavalry company and would probably involve some gun play, not to mention bring the Federal Government down on them, so the idea was abandoned.

It seemed the Castle Gate payroll was a workable heist and the planning was done for the most part during the winter of 1896-97. The topography of Castle Gate was amazing in the Old Days.

Cliffs on both sides of the canyon rose nearly 1000 feet straight up with the Price River, the roadway and the railroad passing through. Very few horses were seen in the area because of the space; there was barely enough room for the shacks the coal miners occupied. There were two ways out of the canyon, up the Price River or down the Price River.

Arrangements were made and the pretty Maude Davis of Vernal, Utah made her way to Robbers Roost near Hanksville, Utah. The mysterious Etta Place was also there. Maude told my mother that Etta was one of the prettiest women she had ever seen and spoke of the walks and talks they shared. Most of that winter, Etta stayed with Butch, Maude and Elzy.

Pearl Baker, Author of THE WILD BUNCH OF ROBBERS ROOST told me of a cabin near the Robbers Roost spring where the initials B.C. and E.P. along with M.D. and E.L. had been carved on a wooden mantle over the fireplace. The cabin burned down many years ago.

Butch and Elzy would ride into the depot area at Castle Gate and hang out. The two cowboys became familiar with the miners and the company store. Butch lounged around the bar and even purchased bottles of Old Crow whiskey on credit. He paid for them later.

Horse racing was very popular on holidays and weekends among the towns of Utah and Colorado.

Butch and Elzy told people they were training race horses particularly for Salt Lake City. The pair would wear some kind of jockey paraphernalia, maybe a colorful shirt or a jockey's helmet, and they had surcingles instead of saddles on their mounts. This was a cover up because they were training the horses to be near the huffing and puffing locomotives of those days.

The mine management was concerned about the threat of a robbery, so the payroll for the miners was delivered on no particular schedule. A signal from the mine whistle let the miners know the payroll was here and it was payday. Butch and Elzy somehow figured this out.

The Pleasant Valley mine office was on the second floor above the company store and was accessible by a set of stairs on the outside of the building. E.L. Carpenter and two employees, a Mr. Phelps and Mr. Lewis came down the stairs and went to the train to pick up the three bags. There was $7,000.00 in one, $1,000.00 in another and $800.00 in silver in the third. When they started up the stairs, Butch was already in place and said "I'll take those" and they were told to put up their hands, Phelps ignored the order and was hit on the head with a pistol. Dazed, he dropped his bag. Elzy was mounted and Butch picked the bags up and tossed them to Elzy, this caused the horse to shy and Butch was afoot. Elzy was able to push Butch's horse against a wall so Butch could mount. They accidentally dropped the bag containing the silver or maybe it was intentional because of its weight. The outlaws stopped behind a shack to exchange their surcingles for saddles and galloped about five miles to where their relay horses were staked out. Mr. Carpenter commandeered a switch engine and headed towards Price, Utah. He stopped to notify the Sheriff, only to find the telegraph line had been cut.

As the outlaws were on the road to Cleveland, Utah, they ran into a mailman who knew Butch and greeted them with a cheery "hello", not knowing about the robbery.

When they reached Buckhorn Draw where another team of relay horses were tied up, the outlaws placed leather coverings on the horse's feet so the posse would have trouble tracking them. A Texan, Joe Walker, a wannabe member of the "Wild Bunch" and one or two other men joined them there. Joe was a Texas cowpuncher who showed up around 1891 in the Price, Utah area. He quickly became acquainted with some of the horse thieves and cattle rustlers. In 1895 or there about, he and another halfwit cowboy tried to take over Price on one of their drunken adventures. They found it to be a bit too big for them. Joe made a habit of harassing the Whitmore's; they raised fine cattle and very well bred horses in the area. Joe claimed to have married one of the Whitmore girls and was entitled to some of the Whitmore family assets. He stole three horses from their ranch at the head of Nine Mile Canyon. A posse was formed, including Sheriff Tuttle, one of the Whitmore's, and two or three other men. The posse surprised Walker and a few shots were fired, one hitting Sheriff Tuttle in the leg. The Sheriff spent the night on the ground and Walker escaped under the cover of darkness. Joe hung around Robbers Roost and became acquainted with some of the

Paymaster E.L. Carpenter,
Courtesy of the Salt Lake Tribune

EL Carpenter
In front of office

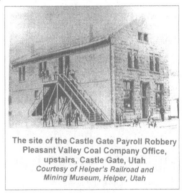

The site of the Castle Gate Payroll Robbery
Pleasant Valley Coal Company Office,
upstairs, Castle Gate, Utah
*Courtesy of Helper's Railroad and
Mining Museum, Helper, Utah*

Pleasant Valley
Coal Company

men around Hanksville and the Roost.

The gang split up and Butch and Elzy kept going south towards Robbers Roost. When the news of the robbery arrived and the law got their bearings, two posses were formed, one out of Emery County and one out of Carbon County. This is quite a while after the outlaws had cleared out.

The two posses spotted one another about dusk and each thought the other were the outlaws. Gunfire started and soon stopped when they realized their mistake. A horse was wounded but not seriously and no member of either posse was injured.

The outlaws made it to Robbers Roost where there was a good deal of safety. One has to know where water and horse feed could be found in this desolate country and very few lawmen ventured into it. Lay split with Butch and went through Torrey, Utah and there attended a dance before going on to Robbers Roost.

With so much time on their hands, how did they spend their days? Did they shoe horses, play cards or have target practice? Yes, all of the above. The outlaws needed some time to celebrate. They stayed around the Roost for some time planning a party. They decided Dixon and Baggs, Wyoming were the places to hold such celebrations. On the 29th of July 1897 they arrived in Dixon, Wyoming just north of the Colorado border, shot up the town harmlessly and went on to Baggs, Wyoming, where they put bullet holes in the walls and ceilings of the bar room. They paid for all the damages in full and the price tag included $1 per bullet hole. The funny part is that most of the townsfolk joined in the fun.

Something interesting happened while the party progressed, Dick Pender of the so called "Powder Springs" gang came down with pneumonia and died. The "Wild Bunch" decided they had a score to settle with the young doctor that had attended Pender. They forced him from his home and held a kangaroo court with Judge John Bennett presiding. Judge Bennett was an ex-con from Arkansas and could neither read nor write. They decided if the doctor was found guilty, he would be hanged. Butch acted as the prosecutor and Elzy the defense. The young doctor thought "this can't be happening!" Something caused a break in the proceedings and the Judge wandered off. The accused was relieved to find out it was all a joke.

The Pleasant Valley Coal Company placed a $2000.00 reward on both Butch and Elzy, and it was later raised to $4000.00, but it was never collected.

Harry Tracy and Dave Lant (no connection to the "Wild Bunch") had escaped from the Utah State Penitentiary around this time, they made their way to Brown's Hole. A posse, that included residents of the area, had the two blocked in a canyon and during this a local man by the name of Valentine Hoy was shot and killed by one of the fugitives. John Bennett, the Judge in the above mentioned trial was caught smuggling food and ammunition to the fugitives. He was taken to the Bassett ranch by a group of men in costumes that hid their identity. They hanged Bennett from the cross piece over the entrance gate of the Bassett ranch. Josie Bassett was about eighteen years of age and her father told her to go into the kitchen so she could not see what was going to take place. Josie told me she had sneaked out and witnessed the whole affair. When it was over, the posse took their costumes off and lo and behold they were all local residents!

What with several train robberies, the area around Brown's Hole was getting too hot for the outlaws. Elzy and Butch left the area and headed for fresh ground in the New Mexico Territory. It should be mentioned that Lay started using the name of his old friend William McGinnis around this time and Cassidy used the name Jim Lowe.

*Harvey Murdock and Mr. & Mrs. D Campbell in 1970 looking
at the cross piece where the hanging took place*

ELZY AND THE KETCHUMS

The association Elzy Lay had with the Ketchum brothers was quite short. Elzy and Butch met the Ketchum brothers while working for the Erie Cattle Company in Alma, New Mexico. Butch did not care for Tom (Black Jack) Ketchum. He thought Sam was more of a man. Butch did not want to see Elzy get mixed up with the Ketchum's and did not want anything to do with them himself.

Butch wanted Elzy to go with him and Sundance to South America. As it turned out, Butch and Sundance left without him and Elzy ultimately ended up in a gun fight at Turkey Creek Canyon where Sam Ketchum and Elzy were both shot by the posse on the 16th of July 1899. Elzy survived but Sam died of blood poisoning the 24th of July 1899.

Sam Ketchum

Tom Ketchum

Ketchum hideout in Turkey Creek

After the robbery of the Colorado and Southern Railroad by Will Carver (aka Charley Franks), Sam Ketchum and William McGinnis (Lay) the fugitives traveled about twenty miles and ended up in Turkey Creek Canyon. Rain and sheep had obliterated their trail. Near evening, the posse had seen a wisp of smoke and surmised it was the Outlaw's camp. The posse was made up of nine or ten men. The names I have are Wilson "Memphis" Elliot, Ed Farr, a Sheriff from Huerfano County, Colorado, W.H. Reno, a detective employed by the Colorado and Southern Railroad, James H. Morgan, Henry M. Love, Perfecto Cordoba, Serna and Frank Smith. Mr. Elliot, deputized by U.S. Marshall Foraker is said to have ordered the crew to open fire if the fugitives did not surrender immediately. Whether McGinnis (Lay) was told to surrender is not known, but as he was headed for a water hole with a canteen, the shooting started. In McGinnis' trial Mr. Cordoba testified that McGinnis was carrying a rifle, but later changed his story. After the gunfight, McGinnis and Carver were able to get Ketchum on his horse and, under the cover of darkness and a heavy rainstorm, traveled about 20 miles before Ketchum could ride no further. He had been hit in the shoulder and his arm was broken below the shoulder. McGinnis and Carver left him and he was found, arrested and taken to prison where he died later as a result of his wound. McGinnis and Carver rode almost the length and width of New Mexico after leaving Ketchum.

Remember that McGinnis had been wounded in the battle and he was sporting four holes in his torso. How they were able to travel at night, acquire food and steal fresh horses while not being captured is nothing short of amazing. They looked for work, but Carver was not known in the area and for obvious reasons, they avoided being seen together. Carver left McGinnis for reasons unknown and headed east to Texas where he was killed in a shootout with lawmen.

McGinnis had all of the loot from the robbery, about $70,000. He rode from near the southern border of Colorado, south to the Mexican border with New Mexico. There he buried the treasure. One historian wrote that he was captured about thirty days later still wearing the same shirt he wore in the gunfight, bullet holes and all. Another school of thought is that he stayed with a young Mexican couple and was very well cared for, probably because he had plenty of money.

Ed Farr and W. H. Reno drawn by Jim Miller

Elzy (McGinnis) was shot two times in his torso. His prison record shows he had scars where both bullets had entered and exited.

With the element of surprise at Turkey Creek Canyon, the battle should have been easy but the inept leadership led to a devastating defeat, both morally and physically. Three members of the posse were killed. Ed Farr died immediately and Mr.'s Love and Smith died later from wounds received in the fight. McGinnis was the first of the outlaws hit by gunfire and was knocked out of the battle.

Mr. Reno walked about twenty miles in the dark to Cimarron, New Mexico seeking help. Fingers were pointed but there was enough blame to go around for the mismanagement of the posse.

The U.S. Marshal, Mr. Creighton Foraker was in charge of the posse at Turkey Creek Canyon, but was not physically present. He tried to place the blame on the members of the posse, however the ineptness of the posse was in Mr. Foraker's self interest.

On the way back from stashing the robbery money in Mexico, McGinnis was invited into breakfast at the Virgil Lusk ranch near Chimney Wells, where he thought he would be safe. The long and short of that is he thought a posse was after him, but they were not. They were after horse thieves. He had one shot left in his pistol. He shot at Lusk and hit him in the wrist, because he thought Lusk turned on him and warned the posse, but that was not the case.

According to some historians, the physical battle that McGinnis put up against extreme odds made quite a tiger out of him. He was very furious and knocked a couple of them unconscious. Finally one of them hit Mac on the head with a pistol and knocked him semi-conscious and they were able to capture him. Lo and behold someone, possibly the sheriff, had a likeness of Elzy Lay or Bill McGinnis, and it was then they realized he was real prize. There was a tremendous reward for the capture of Bill McGinnis, I believe. He and Butch Cassidy had $5000.00 rewards on them, dead or alive.

M. C. STEWART
COMMISSION MERCHANT
OFFICE IN
FIRST NATIONAL BANK BUILDING
DEALER IN ALL KINDS OF LIVE STOCK
CARLSBAD, NEW MEXICO

December 23, 1922.

Mr. E. P. Lamborn,
Leavenworth, Kans.
R. R. No. 2.

Dear Sir:

Yours of the 11th inst. received and contents noted. I am the man who captured William H. McGinus, a member of the Black Jack Gang. In addition to this, I knew several of that gang personally, before they became outlaws. I have a number of memorandums in connection with the operations of the Black Jack Gang during the time they were operating in the Southwest. If I could see you personally and have an interview with you, I am quite sure I could make it worth your while. I have a number of other memorandums in connection with other criminals and bandits who operated in the Southwestern country during the eighteen years I served as sheriff of Eddy County, New Mexico. I have also a number of newspaper clippings that I have preserved and kept all this time and I am sure would interest you.

Hoping to hear from you, I remain,

Yours truly,

B.

M. C. Stewart

Reprint of M.C. Stewart letter of Dec. 23 1922

Mr. E.F. Lamborn
Leavenworth, Kansas
R.R. No. 2
Dear Sir:
Yours of the 11th inst. Received and contents noted. I am the man who captured William H. McGinnis, a member of the Black Jack Gang. In addition to this, I knew several of that gang personally, before they became outlaws. I have a number of memorandums in connection with the operations of the Black Jack Gang during the time they were operating in the Southwest. If I could see you personally and have an interview with you, I am quite sure I could make it worth your while. I have a number of other memorandums in connection with other criminals and bandits who operated in the Southwest country during the eighteen years I served as sheriff of Eddy County, New Mexico. I have also a number of newspaper clippings that I have preserved and kept all this time and I am sure would interest you.

Hoping to hear from you, I remain,

M.C. Stewart

Letter from Sheriff MC Stewart

Cicero Stewart and family

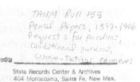
J. Leahy
Attorney at Law
Raton, New Mexico
DISTRICT ATTORNEY
COLFAX & UNION COUNTIES

Raton, N. M., June 14, 1906.

To His Excellency, H.J.Hagerman,

      Governor of New Mexico,

         Santa Fe, New Mexico.

Dear Governor:

      Replying to your favor of the 5th inst., relative to the case of Wm. H. McGinnis, I beg leave to advise you that Wm. H. McGinnis Samuel Ketchum and a man who gave his name as G. W. Franks, on the night of July 11, 1899, held up the C. & S. Southbound train at a point six miles south of Folsom in Union County; that a party of deputy U. S. marshalls, under the direction of Marshall Foraker, located these men in Turkey Canyon, ten miles northwest of Cimarron in this county, about 5 o'clock in the evening of July 16, 1899.; that when they were ordered to throw up their hands they commenced firing on the officers; that two deputy U. S. marshalls, viz., Edward Farr and Henry M. Love were killed, and Sam Ketchum and McGinnis were badly wounded but escaped in the darkness. That on August 16 of the same year M. C. Stewart, sheriff of Eddy County, with two deputies, caught McGinnis by surprise some twenty miles northwest of Carlsbad and captured him. At the September term of court following, the Grand Jury of this county indicted McGinnis for the murder of Dep'ty Farr, and he was tried at the same term, the jury after deliberating some time between first and second degree bringing in a verdict of guilty in the second degree, and on October 10 of the same year he was sentenced to life imprisonment at Santa Fe,.

         Yours very faithfully,

Reprint of J. Leahy letter of June 14, 1906

To His Excellency, H.J. Hagerman

Governor of New Mexico

Santa Fe, New Mexico

Dear Governor:

Replying to your favor of the 5th inst., relative to the case of Wm. H. McGinnis, I beg leave to advise you that Wm. H. McGinnis, Samuel Ketchum and a man who gave his name as G.W. Franks, on the night of July 11, 1899, held up the C. & S. Southbound train at a point six miles south of Folsom in Union County, and robbed the car of same: that a party of U.S. Marshals, under the direction of Marshal Foraker, located these men in Turkey Canyon, ten miles northwest of Cimarron in this county, about 5 o'clock in the evening of July 16, 1899, that when they were ordered to throw up their hands they commenced firing on the officers; that two deputy U.S. marshals, viz., Edward Farr and Henry M. Love were killed, and Sam Ketchum and McGinnis were badly wounded but escaped in the darkness. That on August 16 of the same year M.C. Stewart, sheriff of Eddy County, with two deputies, caught McGinnis by surprise some twenty miles northwest of Carlsbad and captured him. At the September term of court following the Grand Jury of this county indicted McGinnis for the murder of Deputy Farr, and he was tried at the same term, the jury after deliberating some time between first and second degree bringing in a verdict of guilty in the second degree, and on October 10 of the same year he was sentenced to life imprisonment at Santa Fe.

Yours very faithfully,

J. Leahy

Letter from Leahy

One of the most valuable perks of belonging to Western Outlaw and Lawmen Association (WOLA) was getting acquainted with Lawrence Reno, an attorney in Denver, Colorado. He left us in late January, 2008, he will be missed. Larry is the Grandson of William R. Reno who was part of the posse involved in the gunfight at Turkey Creek with my Grandfather. Larry and I spoke often about the uniqueness of our relationship and I have precious memories of him. He said to me "Harv the story of Elzy Lay should be told and you are the one to do it".

At the WOLA gathering in Santa Fe, at Larry's request, we went to the spot where Sam Ketchum's headstone sits very close to El Cerritos Boulevard. This is one of the main arteries of traffic in Santa Fe. Sam's remains are under the highway.

The burial grounds for the prison's indigent were not moved when the highway was built. Along with Bob Pulsipher, Larry insisted we go to the McCubbin residence. Robert McCubbin is the President of the newly merged Western Outlaw and Lawmen History Association. The home is worth a trip to Santa Fe for anyone interested in the history of outlaws and lawmen in the old west. In it one will find a photographic museum that includes anyone and everyone from both sides of the law.

Harvey Murdock and Larry Reno at Sam Ketchum's headstone

Ketchum head stone

Larry and Bob Pulsipher were co-chairs of the WOLA Shootout in Cheyenne, Wyoming held in July of 2007. It was one of the best planned and presented gatherings in WOLA history.

After his capture at the Lusk ranch, McGinnis was taken to Raton, New Mexico and held until they took him to Santa Fe, where he awaited trial.

THE TRIAL

The story about Governor Otero was made possible to a large degree by Meliton Otero. I met Meliton while we were both officiating football games in what was known as the Western Athletic Conference. He and I were officiating two games in Arizona, one at Arizona State in Tempe and the other in Tucson at the University of Arizona. Mel lives in Albuquerque, New Mexico and Otero is a rather common name among Latinos. I asked him if he had any relatives who had been in politics in New Mexico. He told me his Grandfather had been the Governor of the territory in the years around the turn of the century. My reply was "his name was not Miguel Antonio Otero was it?" He responded "how in the world did you know that?" Then I said "He was responsible for pardoning and releasing my Grandfather from the territorial prison at Santa Fe".

Fiesta Bowl 1971
Left Harvey Murdock (forward center) Mel Otero

Governor Otero gives a lengthy account of the trial of William McGinnis. I labored under the thought that Mr. Otero was the Attorney General for the Territory of New Mexico. I was wrong. He served as Territorial Governor from 1897 to 1905. Lays trial and conviction was in October 1899. The Governor sat in on much of the trial. He was quite impressed with McGinnis' testimony. Mr. Otero felt the jury had found McGinnis guilty before the trial began. Mr. Otero is very generous in his evaluation of the conduct and of the presence of mind and courage that McGinnis displayed during the trial. I have a copy of the whole trial from beginning to end and every objection that was presented by the prosecution was sustained, while all of the objections from the defense were overruled.

In those days if a person was found guilty of train robbery or first degree murder, the results were the same. The guilty party could be executed. Had they charged McGinnis with train robbery, he would probably have suffered the same punishment as Tom Ketchum, which was death by hanging. Tom Ketchum was the only man executed under that law.

Governor Otero wrote about this trial in his book "MY NINE YEARS AS GOVERNOR". He wrote about McGinnis' testimony while being questioned on the stand by the prosecuting Attorney. According to Governor Otero, McGinnis said "If the court please, I'm here on trial for murder. I understand there are charges against me for train robbery, another murder and for interfering with the U S Mail. I have been on trial without being given a chance to procure many of my witnesses. I have no way to protect myself and I positively refuse to answer any questions except those asked by the prosecuting attorney, concerning the gunfight."

The jury deliberated for three hours. They brought in a verdict of guilty of murder in the second degree. McGinnis was sentenced to the penitentiary in Santa Fe, New Mexico for the remainder of his natural life.

For a long time I was under the impression that McGinnis was pardoned as a result of his general conduct while in prison. I found out from Larry Reno, the law in those days was the same as it is now. You cannot pardon a lifer. McGinnis had a life sentence and could not have been pardoned.

NEW MEXICO TERRITORIAL PRISON CONVICT RECORD BOOK
RECORD OF WILLIAM H. MCGINNIS

Number:	1348
Name:	William H. McGinnis
When Received:	4 May 1900
Sentence:	Year Life Month -
Term Commenced:	10, October, 1899
Term Expired:	day--- month--- year---
Crime:	Murder
From What County Received:	Colfax
Judicial District:	4th
Judge:	W. J. Mills
Name of Prosecuting Attorney:	J. Leahy
Race:	America
Age:	34
Sex:	Male
Weight:	164
Height:	5 feet 91/2 inches
Eyes:	Lt Brown
Hair:	Light
Complexion:	Light
Size of foot:	5/2
Teeth:	upper tooth broken
Beard Worn:	none
Body Marks:	bullet wound through top left shoulder, bullet marks on ᵇᵒᵗʰ loins, small scar in top of head
Where Born:	Coles Co., Illinois
Occupation:	Laborer
Married or Single:	Single
Children:	None
Religion:	None
Church of Parents:	Methodist
Father Living:	Don't Know
Mother Living:	Don't Know
Age of Self Support:	21
Habits: Temperate	Yes
Intemperate	No
Use Tobacco	Yes
Education: Can Read	Yes
Can Write	Yes
Common School	Yes
High School	No
College	No
Plea at Trial:	Not Guilty
Reasons for Crime:	None
Previous Imprisonment:	None
Nearest Relative or Friend:	E. A. Cunningham, Mogollon, N.M.
Remarks:	Commuted to 10 years by Gov. Otero July 4, 1905 Good Time and Extra Service allowed out Dec. 15, 1905

Reprint of prison record

NEW MEXICO TERRITORIAL PRISON CONVICT
RECORD BOOK
RECORD OF: WILLIAM H. MCGINNIS

Number: 1348
Name: William H. McGinnis
When Received: 4 May 1900
Sentence: Year Life Month
Term Commenced: 10, October, 1899
Term Expired: day---month---year---
Crime: Murder
From What County Received: Colfax
Judicial District: 4th
Judge: W.J. Mills
Name of Prosecuting Attorney: J. Leahy
Race: America
Age: 34
Sex: Male
Weight: 164
Height: 5 feet 9 ½ inches
Eyes: Lt. Brown
Hair: Light
Complexion: Light
Size of foot: 5/2
Teeth: upper tooth broken
Beard Worn: none
Body Marks: bullet wound through top left shoulder,
bullet marks on both loins, small scar on top of head
Where Born: Coles Co., Illinois
Occupation: Laborer
Married or Single:Single
Children: None
Religion:None
Church of Parents: Methodist
Father Living: Don't Know
Mother Living: Don't Know
Age of Self Support: 21
Habits: Temperate   Yes
         Intemperate   No
         Use Tobacco   Yes
Education: Can Read   Yes
           Can Write   Yes
           Common School   Yes

High School   No
College   No
Plea at Trial: Not Guilty
Reasons for Crime;   None
Previous Imprisonment: None
Nearest Relative or friend; E.A. Cunningham, Mogollon, N.M.
Remarks: Commuted to 10 years by Gov. Otero July 4, 1905

Good time and extra service allowed out Dec. 15, 1905

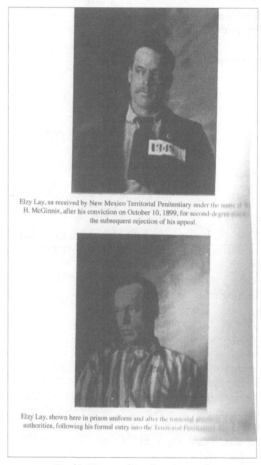

Elzy Lay, as received by New Mexico Territorial Penitentiary under the name of H. McGinnis, after his conviction on October 10, 1899, for second-degree murder, the subsequent rejection of his appeal.

Elzy Lay, shown here in prison uniform and after the territorial prison authorities, following his formal entry into the Territorial Penitentiary.

Double Picture of Lay in prison garb

52

William McGinnis prison mug shot 1899

Because of what he did during his time of incarceration, his sentence was commuted to ten years and he was given consideration for labor that he did. His sentence was further reduced to six years and almost three months.

New Mexico Penitentiary.

Office of Superintendent.

Santa Fe. N. M.,   July 3, 1905.

Dear Sir:-

As it is the custom with you to issue a pardon or commutation
to some deserving inmate of the Penitentiary on the Fourth of July, I
desire to recommend for your consideration William H. McGinnis, who was
sentenced from Colfax County October 10th, 1899 for life for the crime
of murder.   At the present time he is confined to his bed with inflamator y
rheumatism and has been a sufferer from the same for quite awhile.
He has been a model prisoner in every sense of the word and during his
entire imprisonment not a single mark has been placed against him.   He
has rendered the institution valuable services.   Three years as head
engineer in our brick department and the balance of the time as stewart,
taking as much interest in his work as any paid employee could do.
We beleive that if you should see proper to release or commute him that
he will make a good and law abiding citizen.

Respectfully yours,

Hon. M. A. Otero,

Governor of New Mexico,

Santa Fe., New Mexico.

Superintendent,

Reprint of Olaf Bursum letter July 3, 1905
Hon. M.A. Otero
Governor of New Mexico,
Santa Fe, New Mexico.
Dear Sir:
As it is the custom with you to issue a pardon or commutation to
some deserving inmate of the
 Penitentiary on the Fourth of July, I desire to recommend for your
consideration William H. McGinnis,
Who was sentenced from Colfax County October 10th, 1899 for
life for the crime of murder. At the
 Present time he is confined to his bed with inflammatory
rheumatism and has been a sufferer of the
 same for quite awhile.
He has been a model prisoner in every sense of the word and during
his entire imprisonment and not a

54

Single mark has been placed against him. He has rendered the institution valuable services. Three years
as Head engineer in our brick department and the balance of the time as steward, taking as much
interest in his work as any paid employee could do. We believe that if you should see proper to release
or commute him that he will make a good and law abiding citizen.
Respectfully yours,
H.O. Bursum
Superintendent

Letter from H Olaf Bursum

New Mexico Prison Superintendent Holm Olaf Bursum. After Elzy Lay helped out during two separate prison breaks, Bursum supported Lay's efforts aimed at obtaining a pardon. *Courtesy Holm Olaf Bursum III.*

Superintendent Olaf Bursum

Reprint of Governor Otero document July 3, 1905
EXECUTIVE OFFICE
Santa Fe, N.M. July 3, 1905
WHEREAS, At the regular October A.D. 1899 term of the
district court sitting within and for the county
Of Colfax, Territory of New Mexico, William H. McGinnis was
convicted and sentenced to the Territorial
Penitentiary; and
WHEREAS, The authorities at the Territorial Penitentiary
recommend that a commutation be granted
In this case, and state that McGinnis has been a most exemplary
prisoner, that his conduct has been
excellent during the entire period of his imprisonment; and
WHEREAS, it has become the general custom on each fourth day

56

of July, the anniversary of our independence, to extend executive clemency, to some poor unfortunate:

NOW THEREFORE, I, MIGUEL A. OTERO, Governor of the Territory of New Mexico, by virtue of the authority in me vested, after carefully reviewing the case of said prisoner, William H. McGinnis

Find that he is worthy of executive clemency, and do this day commute his sentence to a term of ten years from its date; and the superintendant of the Territorial Penitentiary upon receipt of this executive order properly signed and sealed, will act in accordance therewith.

Done at the Executive Office this the 3rd day of July, A.D. 1905
WITNESS MY HAND AND THE GREAT SEAL OF THE TERRITORY OF NEW MEXICO.

Miguel A. Otero

Letter from Miguel Otero

Reprint of McGinnis letter of July 6, 1905
Santa Fe, New Mexico
July 6, 1905
To His Excellency,
M.A. Otero
Governor of New Mexico
Dear Governor:
I beg leave to address you and offer a humble apology for my apparent
indifference and ungratefulness
in not expressing at once my thanks and gratitude to you for your

extreme kindness in granting to me
a commutation of sentence.

Let me assure you Dear Governor that I was so overcome by my emotions of joy and happiness at the near approach of liberty that I was unable to make speech of any kind befitting the occasion.

It has been said, "Out of the fullness of the heart the mouth speaketh" but another hath said "out of the fullness of the heart the soul overfloweth and man is lost to reason". The latter condition was mine, therefore I now seek this opportunity to express my sincere thanks and deepest gratitude to you for your kindness to me, and your expression of confidence that I would never cause you any further trouble. You have made no mistake Governor and may the richest of Heavens blessings fall upon you and yours with many more years of honor and happiness is the sincere wish of one whose feet you have just placed on the road that leads to success and happiness. In conclusion let me assure you I shall use my utmost endeavors not to betray the trust you have placed in me and I shall exert myself to the extent of my ability to become an honorable and useful citizen and one to whom you can point to with pride. Dear Governor, words are not adequate to express my gratitude. Please accept my thanks and humble apology and believe me ever your humble and grateful friend.

Very respectfully yours,
William H. McGinnis
P.S. I would like an interview with you before the expiration of my sentence.

Letter from McGinniss

I will take the part of the devil's advocate and express my opinion on his commutation. Remember that McGinnis had about $70,000.00 and no one to share it with. He had it buried along the border with Old Mexico. Will Carver was dead and Sam Ketchum was dead. That made it all his. That was a tremendous amount of money in those days. McGinnis had strong motivation to behave himself while in prison. He became a trustee to the extent of managing the electrical plant for the penitentiary. He also carried mail into Santa Fe from the penitentiary and often times carried the payroll from Santa Fe to the penitentiary. It wasn't very far but it showed he was a pretty good citizen while in prison.

A man by the name of Olaf Bursum, who later became a senator for New Mexico, was the warden at the Santa Fe prison while McGinnis was there. In his recollections of McGinnis, Bursum's wife credits McGinnis for saving the life of her younger brother while in the living quarters of the officers housing area. He was captured by some of the lifers. McGinnis was able to talk the prisoners out of the idea of keeping the hostage. Mrs. Bursum was sure McGinnis had saved a life.

Another time the night bakers were being escorted from their cells to the culinary area when they over powered the guard and took his keys to the weapons cache. They were able to get a hold of weapons. McGinnis was called by Mrs. Bursum, he mounted a horse and rode to Santa Fe in the dark. He was able to get a group of military personal to come out to the prison. The Cavalry was able to put down the uprising without any casualties.

McGinnis' official records show that his sentence was commuted the third of July 1905 but he was released on Christmas Eve 1905. It was policy in those days to release prisoners on Independence Day and Christmas Day.

He went from Santa Fe to Alma, New Mexico which as discussed earlier, he and Butch Cassidy worked on the W.S. ranch. McGinnis stayed with a pair of brothers who ran a store in the area. When the store needed change or small amounts of money, McGinnis would supply it for them. He stayed around there for a couple of months.

Alma, New Mexico is south of Santa Fe, close to the Mexican border and McGinnis (Lay) was known around Alma when he was training horses for the W.S. Ranch. He was known as "Mac" and for about two months, stayed around Alma. Then he decided to go back to Brown's Hole and Baggs, Wyoming.

HEADING HOME

For years he wondered about Maude Davis and their daughter, Marvel. He went to Vernal, Utah and found that Maude had married Oran L. Curry and Lay's daughter was going by the name of Marvel Curry (no relation to "Kid Curry" of the "Wild Bunch").

*Maude and daughter
Marvel Curry*

It is debatable that Maude and Elzy were ever legally married, but for the sake of argument this was Maude's second marriage. Lay did not contact them at that time but continued on to Baggs, Wyoming. Sometime later he went back to Vernal to get acquainted with his daughter.

She was attending The Wilcox Academy, and was in her early teens. Lay had been working on one of the Calvert ranches. When he found his daughter, she took back her real name of Lay. She graduated from The Wilcox Academy on the 1st of June 1917 under the name of Marvel Matilda Lay. She told me of her love for Papa Curry but stayed in touch with her real father from then on. Lay attended her graduation in Vernal. Maude was married three times after Lay. Oran Liddiard Curry, together they had two sons, O.E. and Allen. John Samuel McDougall, they had one son, Edward. Albert Benton Atwood, Albert B. came from that union. Maude lived thirty seven years as a widow.

Mac took back his real name while working for Kirk Calvert. He married Mary Calvert on the 23rd of March 1909. The Marriage License reads William Ellsworth Lay and Mary Calvert and was performed in Thermopolis, Wyoming, witnessed by Mr. and Mrs. Tom Skinner. Lay was 39 years and Mary was 22 years of age. Two children came from that marriage, a son James and a daughter Mary Lucille. Many of his friends continued to call him Mac for the rest of his life.

Lay family reunion in Iowa sometime between 1919 and 1920. Elzy Lay in tie Marvel Lay Murdock holding her daughter

Lycurgus Calvert (Kirk)

Kirk was a lead member of the survey crew that staked out the Union Pacific section of the trans-continental railroad between Omaha, Nebraska and Salt Lake City, Utah. After the job was complete, he went back to the area around Rawlins and Baggs, Wyoming. He was very successful and set a goal for himself of starting a cattle ranch for each of his children. He achieved this goal.

Kirk Calvert became a deputy sheriff in Rawlins, Wyoming and was later elected sheriff in Baggs, Wyoming. This was around the time the loosely knit "Wild Bunch" was starting to establish a reputation. As earlier mentioned this label was used by the Pinkerton's and the name stuck.

There was a bad hombre called Big Nose George Parrott, he was not involved with any of the "Wild Bunch", Big Nose was simply a bad man. Kirk Calvert captured him and had him in jail awaiting trial. Some of the locals took matters into their own hands and built a scaffold. They were in the process of hanging Big Nose when the scaffold broke, so they just shot him. The mortician partially skinned him and a wallet and a pair of moccasins were made from Georges' hide. They were on display in Rawlins for a long time. Sheriff Calvert received a $3000.00 reward and given a lifetime Pass on the Union Pacific railroad.

Although Lay worked on the Calvert ranches, he was not a cowboy, and did not like the daybreak to dark work and drudgery of breeding information, bookkeeping, and the hiring and firing of cowboys.

As has been mentioned, Elzy had a drifter spirit. Even though he was a married man with children, he felt the need to roam. He started going to town often. There he would visit a man by the name of Ian Maupin. Ian repaired the new

gasoline engine cars that began to be more numer-
ous every year.

From left to right children
Lloyd Calvert, Mary Calvert Lay, Ada Calvert Piper, and dad Kirk Calvert

The Calvert Family

James and Lucille Lay. The children of Elzy Lay and Mary Calvert

Maupin was also an employee of the Baggs branch of the Rawlins Bank. Elzy had a real knack for learning and really enjoyed being in the shop with Ian. The two became close friends. After a while Elzy would accompany Ian from Baggs to the bank in Rawlins, Wyoming with cash and securities. At first townspeople told Ian he was crazy to trust this ex-con anywhere around bank money. Ian didn't think twice about Elzy. He told anyone who voiced his or her concern that Elzy was a trusted friend and the bank's money was safe. Elzy became Ian's guard on those 50 mile rides to the bank in Rawlins. Elzy told Ian stories of his past and the two built a bond of knowledge and trust.

THE OILMAN

In 1910 oil fever swept across Wyoming. Professor Boyle, a professor of geology from Yale University was hired by Union Pacific and came to Baggs looking for a guide into the backcountry of the area. He was looking at the possibility of finding a good location for oil discovery. He contacted Ian Maupin in hopes of finding a good guide. Ian told him of Elzy Lay. Ian could not think of anyone who knew the area better than his friend and he knew that his friend was beginning to get the itch to roam. Professor Boyle showed interest in meeting Elzy, so Ian made sure all of the cards were on the table. He told the professor that Elzy was incarcerated for murder in New Mexico and was a member of the infamous Wild Bunch. Ian also let the professor know that there was no one he trusted more. A meeting was set up at the Baggs bank. It didn't take long for Professor Boyle to know that Elzy was going to be the perfect guide. They left together two days later on an oil seeking expedition.

A few weeks after Elzy and the professor left Baggs, Elzy came back to town for supplies. Ian had never seen him happier. He asked Elzy about the job he was doing and Elzy told his friend of all the things the professor was teaching him. He was alive with excitement. He was being taught the science of geology around the campfire at night with as much effort as if he were in a classroom at Yale. The professor was very impressed with Elzy's intelligence and went as far as ordering several books for Elzy, to assist him with his quest for knowledge. Every few weeks Elzy would return to town for supplies and talked of geology and nothing else. Ian was very pleased to see his friend so passionate about something.

The expedition ended in the fall of that year, Elzy and the professor said their goodbyes. A bond of friendship was certainly carved from their months together and common interests. The Professor found an enthusiastic student and the student had found something to be interested in, which he had not found since his outlaw days. Elzy Lay had definitely been bitten by the oil bug. During that summer Elzy spent very little time at home with his family. This would be a pattern his family would see often during the remainder of his life.

Later; in the fall of 1916, Elzy made the decision to prospect for oil. He told his friend Ian he was heading to the Powder Wash country to look for oil. He left one day with a packhorse loaded with supplies heading for a new adventure. Alone in the backcountry of Wyoming was the perfect life for this former outlaw. Now instead of hiding from lawmen in the hills he knew so well, he was happily analyzing rock formations for any sign of oil. He had as much knowledge of what to look for as any college educated geologist.

In October Elzy returned to Baggs in the middle of the night. He called on his friend Ian, too excited to wait until morning. He was black from head to toe from the oil shale he had found. He told Ian he had had a strike in the Vermillion Creek area just 70 miles southeast of Rock Springs, Wyoming. "It looks like a big field," he told his friend. Elzy wanted Ian to be his partner. They talked long and hard that night. Ian said he knew of a couple of guys who would make good partners. Wif Wilson and W.H. Coats were experts in mining and could be invaluable since they would know how to get the oil out. Elzy agreed and in a few days the four men got together and an oil company was formed. Elzy, then wanted to show his new partners the area he had discovered.

In the months to follow, Wilson, Coates and Lay worked in the Vermillion Creek area to stake their claims. As the trio went throughout the area staking and collecting data, Maupin would take the data to the County Clerk in Green River, Wyoming to be recorded. The men managed to stake the entire field twelve miles long and six miles wide. In those days everything was done on foot and on horseback so you can imagine how labor intensive the job was. The way a claim was kept back then was that $100.00 worth of work would need to be done on the claim each year. It was called proving up the claim.

After they had completed the initial work, they went looking for financial backing to work on getting the oil. In order to get financial backing, a certified geologist was going to have to verify there was oil in the area. The group of men enlisted the help of a geologist who, after seeing the claim, reported to the financial backers that Elzy had found the perfect oil structure, but that the oil was too deep and getting it out would be nearly impossible. This was not good news for the small company that had put so much effort in the project. The men did not lose faith and decided to hire another geologist for a second opinion. Unfortunately, the second geologist concurred with the first and reported that the oil would be nearly impossible to reach. The group was not willing to give up and, believing in Elzy's conviction that there was a large deposit of oil in the field, decided to go after it. They chose one of their stakes, one Elzy felt sure about, and began to drill for oil. Days turned to months and months turned to years and the group was running out of funds and backers with funds.

Unfortunately for the mining group, there was an amendment to the Placer Mining Act that passed in 1920. The amendment made certain non-metallic minerals such as petroleum and oil shale not open for claim staking. Since claims could no longer be secured, stakes became government lands that were required to be leased. When it came time to lease the land that the small oil company had been working, a decision had to be made. The men were tired and disheartened. After a great deal of discussion, Coats decided to give up and move to Mexico to mine for another company. Maupin had obligations in town with his shop and opted out of the oil business.

Wilson really wanted Lay to continue drilling with him. Elzy was tired and had lost faith. He began to believe that the oil was not reachable. He had his family and he could go back to running the ranch, so he declined Wilson's offer. He rode away slightly defeated, as he had been so sure oil was under that spot. Wilson was convinced Elzy was right and refused to give up. He leased the land where they had been drilling and went east to find new backers. He found a wildcat oil operation that was willing to get the oil and got some financial backing. The new crew set up to drill. Though the oilmen of this new operation felt there may be a better spot farther down from where the original group had tried, Wilson was adamant that the crews drill on the spot Elzy had originally showed Wilson. The crew set up the rig and began to drill. The equipment must have been superior to the equipment used by Lay's group, as it was not long before they discovered natural gas.

Word spread that gas had been found in the Vermillion Creek area. When asked, Lay would sadly smile and announce that he knew he had been right about oil being there because his teacher was too good not to have taught him well.

The oil field became one of the largest in the west. Unfortunately Elzy Lay received nothing except for one entry on the books for a claim signed William McGinnis. The field is still in production today. It is known as the Hiawatha dome and there is a tremendous gas field and transmission lines that deliver natural gas to Salt Lake City and Ogden, Utah. Life certainly has its turns.

After awhile, he became quite restless again. Mary's father asked Elzy and Mary to stay in Baggs and help run the ranch, but Elzy was not a cowboy. He started going over to the Shoshone area where he gambled and managed saloons.

Elza Lay -- outlaw, geologist -- developed oil and gas area

Special to the Express
By Kerry Ross Boren

If anyone in the Uintah Basin were asked,

"Who was Elza Lay?" they would very likely quickly say, "He was an outlaw -- a member of the Wild Bunch". In this they would be correct, but few persons are aware that Elza Lay played another much more important part in the history of this region.

ELZA LAY was born William Ellsworth Lay in McArthur, Vinton County, Ohio November 25, 1871, a son of James Landon and Mary Jane (Ballew) Lay. When still a child, "Elza" went with his parents to Phillips County, Kansas and later to Wray, Colorado. At the age of 13, Lay left home and first appeared in Brown's Park north of Vernal in 1888 where he went to work for Matt Warner on Diamond Mountain.

Elza Lay's career grew rapidly from that time forth. Making an early acquaintance of Butch Cassidy, Elza soon became known as one of the most famous (or infamous) outlaws of the Wild Bunch. Not the least of his many accomplishments in this field or work was his participation in the Montpelier bank Robbery, the Castle Gate Payroll Robbery and the Wilcox Train Robbery, all within the course of

FIRST OIL WELL in Clay Basin. Man in center is Elza Lay, influential in development of oil and gas industry in Utah, Wyoming and Colorado.

Article from the Vernal Express; The caption read
FIRST OIL WELL in clay basin. Man in center is Elzy Lay, influential in
development in oil and gas industry in Utah, Wyoming & Colorado.

OFF TO CALIFORNIA

He became disheartened with the whole area, and even though it was a good life for his family in Baggs, he decided to go to southern California. He gained employment as a manager on the irrigation system in the Imperial Valley. He lived in Calexico on the border of California and Mexico. Mary went out and lived with him for some time, but it was a miserable existence out there because it was very hot without air conditioning. She went back and forth between Glendale California and Calexico. Several years ago I did a piece for Dick and Daun DeJournette in their book, 100 YEARS IN BROWN'S PARK

AND DIAMOND MOUNTAIN. I told my Aunt Lucille (Elzy and Mary's daughter) what I was doing. She thought it was fine to do it but she said to me "Please leave me out of it." I couldn't understand why until I had a long talk with her. She did not know that until after his death her dad had been incarcerated, which she discovered as she and her mother were going through his papers. She confided in me that she was devastated and disappointed when she made that discovery.

Elzy's application for the Imperial Irrigation District

While he was managing the irrigation company, his entire workforce was Mexican. He picked up the Spanish language quickly. In addition to his responsibilities, he would handle their money, purchase their clothing and do favors for them, because he was fluent in their language. All of these things were easy and he earned their trust and gained their loyalty. His ability to educate himself over and over again was remarkable.

Lucille was a very kind and loving daughter. She and my mother were so much alike in that respect. I wanted to ask her about taking care of Lay during his last days. She said he was an excellent patient, he never complained, he was very gracious, thankful for food that had been prepared. I never had the courage to ask her if she had seen his torso while taking care of him. He had to have four terrible scars from the bullets from the Turkey Creek gunfight. As mentioned earlier, both bullets had entered and exited, one on the shoulder and one on the hip.

In my conversations with Lucille, I grew to understand how difficult Lay's life was in the last days. He was afflicted with asthma and had a problem with alcohol. He would leave, sometimes for months at a time. I'm not sure how many times, but once was more than two or three years. It was rumored he went to South America to check on his friend Butch, but of course this cannot be verified. During this time he was under the influence of alcohol, which was extremely bad and Lucille was broken hearted about it. This left Mary in a tough spot with a couple of kids, and she moved back to Wyoming where Lucille attended school. She was back and forth a few times and was not living a very good life. Lucille's childhood and school days were particularly hard. After growing up, she began working in a Ford agency where she learned the business quite well. Someone needed to, because the owner spent more time on the golf course than in his dealership. Lucille, for all intents and purposes ran the show. She went on from there to the investment banking business where she spent the rest of her professional life. She was very successful.

Mary Calvert Lay with children James and Lucille

She married Ralph Morgan who was with Paramount Studios. That is how Lay got into motion

Lay head stone

Ralph Morgan

pictures featuring Tom Mix, Johnny Mac Brown, Randolph Scott and other cowboys of the silver screen era. This is purely speculation on my part, but it is possible that Lay was acquainted with the famous Lawman Wyatt Earp. I say this because Tom Mix was a pallbearer at Earp's funeral.

Elzy Lay in black hat on a movie set

Ralph and Lucille did not have any children, however, her brother James Lay had two or three children whom I have lost track of. After Elzy died, James visited my mother in Heber City. It was the only time I ever saw him.

I remember Lay coming to our home in Heber City twice and Mary was with him each time. One recollection of his visits is my curiosity about him not going to bed. I learned then about his asthma, which prevented him from sleeping in bed, lying down. On his visits, he would take all the kids swimming at the Homestead in Midway, west of Heber City Utah.

My Grandfather died in Glendale, California on Nov. 10, 1934. He is interred in the Forest Lawn cemetery in the Los Angeles area. I was nine years of age.